LIRA'S
LYRICS

YOUR POWER HELPS YOUR THROE

Mike Lira

Order this book online at www.trafford.com
or email orders@trafford.com

Most Trafford titles are also available at major online book retailers.

Printed in the United States of America.

ISBN: 978-1-4269-7919-4 (sc)
ISBN: 978-1-4269-7920-0 (e)

Trafford rev. 02/22/2012

 www.trafford.com

North America & international
toll-free: 1 888 232 4444 (USA & Canada)
phone: 250 383 6864 ♦ fax: 812 355 4082

CONTENTS

SELF WORTH

I went to a party to have a blast
Took some speed to make the night last
I saved my whisky and drank cold beer
Looked around to see who was here
A lot of dudes and chicks around
Whiskey beer and drugs was easily found
There was a crowd in one corner I saw
Sniffing in dope through a straw
Drinking and music was going on
I was hoping the night was never gone
One by one people passed out fast
I thought by taking speed I would last
I used my conscious to do what was right
Walking swiftly away I made my flight
I thought I had better use myself worth
Wishing I had that good thinking from birth
Thinking it over I am sure I will stay home
And find a better place to roam

SLIPPERY

By being sober I know
Slippery places I will not go
Temptation will always be around
It won't bother you if sobriety is found

INSPIRE

Be happy for sun or rain today
Have your "Power" lead you the way
Going to a meeting is good
You know you're doing what you should
At meetings everything we discuss
Problems are helped for all of us
Joys you have we all like to hear
It is wonderful to share to a peer
Bad thing define good
So do what you should
Stay sober and you will know
It is the best way to go
Joy is intensified by sorrow
Be happy today forget tomorrow
Loneliness does make love
Just ask your "Power" above
Inspire another with a turn about
We will have a reason to shout
Staying sober you will win
You'll be happy once more again

LIGHT

Entire satisfaction never came with alcohol
Using, drinking is hard to accomplish anything at all
Thinking it would bring me relief
I found was a wrong belief
My attitude and thinking was very wrong
I felt alone and didn't belong
Being sober I'd never be true
I was wrong in all I would do
My life I couldn't control
I had nothing good in my soul
I had turn my life around
Getting sober I was broke

I was sick, lonesome and wanted to croak
AA living I happily changed my mind
Everything I do get better I find
If you or anyone starts to feels like I did
Start a new life for AA will open the jar with tight lid
Satisfaction comes when you are happy and healthy
Being drunk I never got wealthy
I just want to live life right
Being sober the light shines bright

PEACE

NA, AA, and the Bible are alike a lot
The books don't believe in drugs alcohol or pot
In Matthew there is 9 blessings in chapter 5
They bless you while you are still alive
In NA and AA there are steps to help us think
The books tell us not to use or drink
The books have a spirit for us to find
It picks us up from the awful grind
Crying in church or meetings we can do
No one will think badly of you
Following the Bible or Big Book if we are meek
We will prosper each day month or week
Hunger and thirsting for doing good will be done
Our blessings of temptation will be won
If we are merciful, mercy we get back
Happiness comes when we are on the right track

To see God you are blessed with a pure heart
We will love together with him and never part
With peace we will be his son
Living in heavens is what we won
Being persecuted for living right
We will never be out of his sight
We are blessed by not talking evil but good
It should be known and simply understood
The books do teach us how to live
Follow what they say and teach how to give
In James 1:12 if temptation you can endure
You are blessed with God's crown of life for sure

ANGER

Anger is a topic we talk about a lot
Anger is something we all got
We wonder how to stop that pain
By letting it go peace we gain
Anger makes us say and do wrong
It is very hard to get along
We all think different the way we feel
So ask you power to make things real
Get rid of angers fear
Know your power is near
Staying sober it is clear to say
We can send anger on its way

ATTITUDE

Our attitude is how we think
It is good when we don't drink
People can see and hear it in your talk
It is there when you move or walk
It expresses itself in everything
With sobriety peace it will bring
A positive attitude get things done well
Being negative you are not able to tell
Being positive problems are solved with control
It makes you feel good in your soul
Be strong and refuse defeat
Show yourself addiction you can beat

MY CHOICE

I drank a lot for my family is that way
That is what society and friends say
Life's surrounding and environment makes my
Decision agree
But do I want this kind of life being for me!
If I want freedom I must believe it isn't so
The way I believe and decide is the way I will go
I choose and want to be living in recovery
Now my friends and society think different of me

THE PROGRAM

The program offers freedom as a gift
It gave my happiness and health a lift
Accepting my addiction was the key
That is the way I want my life to be
There are things I cannot change
But my addiction I can rearrange
Accepting my addiction I will do
Now the mistakes I make will be few
By changing my behavior I will win
And I must not go to my old behavior again

Months

January starts a brand new year
With AA-n-NA you can shed your fear
February it seems Love you find
When attending meetings you are in our mind
March is the first sign of spring
Meetings welcome all friends you bring
April there are stories to read
They give a lot of your sobriety's need
May's sobriety fragrant smell
Gives you a great sober yell
June when we see the full moon
Promises will be yours soon
July we are sober half that year

Not having to think of any fear
August is for all young and old
Meetings are helpful when your story is told
September harvest is in full swing
Love is what sobriety will bring
October you can read the "Big Book" over
You'll find the reasons to stay sober
November be thankful for AA-n-NA
Live it always day by day
December you've had sobriety all year
That is what everyone wants to hear

STEP

The steps open my eyes to see
What is all happening to me
I learn what is bad and good
So I can do and spread what I should
The truth will stay in my mind and sight
Being able to know, do and think right
Your "Higher Power" will not lead you wrong
I know for sure He is with us all day long
Doing and spreading a step each day
Gets better to have sobriety in us stay

Admitting

Admitting you're an alcoholic, you're not defeated
For your life is not yet totally completed
For there is now new things for you
To succeed find all you must do
Getting sober is a must at all cost
Surely you will find all that you have lost
During the holidays get stronger
Make your sobriety last longer
If temptation happens to come to pest
Have your "higher Power" put temptation to rest
Your life is a very important one
So stay sober until your life is done

CONCERN

Out of all the things I always yearn
Sobriety today is my main concern

LICK IT

When I was drinking I thought I was having a sensation
Broke coming home I had no explanation
That was the way I broke my loves relation
I woke up with a bad attitude and very sick
My head hurt feeling like I got hit with a brick
This way of living I knew I had to lick
Sobriety I found gave me another chance
My attitude changed, so did my romance
Now my life and family I can enhance
I no longer wonder on what I should do
Sobriety in my heart opened and grew
It is simple and is there for me and you

GOALS

Setting a goal, perfection is our strife
Everyone wants that in their life
Getting frustration and despair if our goal's not there
Yield to reality, for perfection is rare
Reasonable goals you must learn to set
For those are the one you will get
Parts of big goals you have won
Doing so you did have fun
Being sober having a clear mind
Your goals are easier to get, you'll find
Day to day year after year
Sobriety takes away shame guilt and fear
Having sobriety in my life and heart
Has given me a new meaningful start

HUMBLE

Being jealous and having envy of others is hard to get
Out of my mind
I get hateful, mean and it is hard to control myself I find
People with money, beauty and material things I wished
I possessed
Is what I must not want and I should put it to rest
Learning to be satisfied of what I have and can do
Must stick in my mind like Elmer's glue
Maybe you have what others wish they had
I am sure they can overcome being mad
Prayer to a power helps them and also you
Humbling yourself is one thing you should do.

BEST WAY

Being sober every single day
You will find is the best way

VIEW

Liking myself best I will try
There are so many reasons why
Without myself there is no one
I'd not be alive to have any fun
Getting drunk I am not very sincere
I have a temper not wanting any one near
Wrong things I say and do
People I like are very few
Being sober I have a different point of view
I see good points in all of you
Loving things is easier to do
A sober life is happier for me and you

NEED

First coming to AA I was confused but felt great
I received a lot of love controlling unwanted hate
Blessings came and I thought I should share
All my friends in the program really care
Living in sobriety is our life's need
It gives us happiness taking away greed
We all have our choice to take
Living the Big Book is not at all fake

SHARE

AA enjoys everyone when they share
Whatever the situation AA will help and care

WITH IN

From within happiness will come
Sobriety is best for all not just some
Happiness is extending your hand and caring
A parent or teacher it comes from sharing
Demonstrate your joy by actions
You will see wonderful reactions
Living in sobriety is the only way
When you accept the brand new day
Temptation is dangerous when you're egged on
With faith and self will it will be gone
The reason my happiness grew
Is "I had my sobriety" continue
Promises and new beginning is now here
It keeps my happiness and takes away my fear

THE SEED

It is hard when things don't go your way
That is the time when I pray
With AA I'm pulled out of the hole
Evil thoughts I try to control
It's nice when we live like we should
Sobriety happens when you are doing good
It may be hard as time goes on
For evil will never be gone
The "Big Book" will plant the seed
It will feed you what you need
At meetings we have a force
Our "Higher Power" leads our course
Things in life we are able to endure
It is too hard without sobriety I am sure
Being sober until life's end
Makes my life and troubles easier to mend

DESIRE

Taking my first drink of hard liquor
My throat burned my face made a snicker
I felt strong all over and became warm
I thought I had power over any harm
Chances I took were out of control
I cheated lied and even stole
Life was hard when time went on
My health was bad my mind almost gone
I went to jail before too long
Living for liquor I found was all wrong
Happy, I was able to find a new way
It was to stay sober every day
The "Big Book" helps solve a situation
It will help anyone in any nation
I found a "Power" that is up higher
It changed liquor to another desire
Having sobriety each morning all day
Is the best way to live I now must say

THINKING

Never being able to stop an addiction don't say
It just might be harder to do today
Evil thinking wants your thinking to linger on
But not giving up addiction will be gone
Death with addiction is bound to be
So keep on trying to be addiction free

THE POWER

Begin each day thinking of Higher Power
Will help you through each day's hour
Praying in mind and heart
My Power gives me wonderful start
I will stay in tuned with him today
Evil in me there will be no way
Praying redirects my mind
Letting me realize what to find
As I let the power in me flow
Evil temptation around me has to go
There is no separation with my power today
Having the Power with me on break, lunch, all day
The light in life's tunnel will not fade away

RESPECT

Drinking or using there is so much lost
Doing so I didn't realize the cost
Friends, freedom and respect fade away
When I drank or used any day
These problems I knew I had to overcome
The joys in the "Big Book" made me want some
The twelve steps over and over I must do
For they are written for alcoholics like me and you
The best thing to do is refuse
When asked to drink or use
Staying sober today is a wonderful thing
Life, freedom and health it will bring
By staying sober "Just for today"
For all of us is the best way

FREEDOM

Freedom is available for all who want it
It's easier done when wrong doing you quit
Your choice is there to choose
Stay sober and don't use
New priorities give a wonderful start
Never let and your "Power" part
Freedom from chemicals and booze
Doing so you won't lose
Have a life that is clean
By prayer Evil won't be seen

DO NOT FAIL

Consuming alcohol and drugs I fail
That is the reason I have been to jail
In the hospital I have been
If I relapse I will go again
Overdosing I will surely die
Everyone will know the reason why
With sobriety and no relapse I will win
I will stay happy enjoying life again
Not drinking I know I am living
I know so these words I am giving
By knowing that I'll stay living that way
Even if it is just for today

It is important not to slip
Don't even take little nip
Alcohol gives you different faces
So you must avoid slippery places
Everyone knows when you are hooked
It leads you to be broke or booked
A higher power won't lead you astray
It will keep you sober day by day
Living the "Big Book" when you read
Will plant a fruitful life we all need

PROBLEMS

When I rank and drugged problems were not over
I know it is better in life by staying sober
Drinking it is easier to lose a life freedom or mind
By being sober it is easier to get out of a bind
Be truthful in all things you say
The outcome is easier on you that way
You heal faster when you get a cut or bruise
So say NO if asked to drink or use
It is best to stay away from evil temptation
Using and abusing gives you the wrong sensation
If you want a high do it sober with love
You'll be soaring like a dove

SITUATIONS

When I was drinking situations went wrong
I was sick lonely and broke before too long
Feeling I had to get away from the crowd
I quit drinking and inside I was proud
People didn't think I could stop for long
I had to prove to myself they were wrong
Giving up the bondage of alcohol I feel free
I was now being who I wanted to be
I know it is easy when I keep in my mind
There is not much hardship when I leave it behind
Sometimes you think things are wrong
Situations like that don't stay long
Good things for you end the right way
That is why I live sober day by day

GRIEF

Time and life is wasted by storing up grief
Learning to handle them brings relief
Grudges injustice, and out downs are hard to overcome
Forgetting and forgiving is real hard for some
With love and compassion things fall into place
Life is no longer hard to face

Effects

Alcohol can be treacherous or good
A doctor uses it like he should
Using it to get rid of infections you may get
But to get intoxicated, you must quit
It's really not how or what when you think
Your mind and body don't function right
In the end there is no light
When realizing you're an addict and admit
Continue on, for that will be suing your wit
You have a choice to be addiction free
And that's the way all of us want to be

LIVE

Be glad you are awake
Live sober for goodness sake
There is no reason to drink or use
If you do it you light a fuse
You'll go out with a big bang
There'll no longer be "The Gang"
Usually you are sick or in jail
Doing those things you only fail
Be glad there is AA to go
You'll learn the right things to know
Ourselves or others we can cry or pray
So be grateful just for today
There are so many things you can have in life
Whether it is family children or wife
No matter what things we must face
Staying sober you'll be in the right place

THE RIGHT PATH

In this world of so many things wrong
Finding the right path don't take long
It depends on mostly where you look
You'll do right following the "Big Book"
It is like compass showing the right direction
What also helps is reading our "Daily Reflection"
Go to meetings and you'll receive a treat
For it is you and I are the people you'll meet

Printed in the United States
By Bookmasters